Photo Credits

i	Donald Newmeyer. Los Angeles. CA. 1951
	Clown photographs: Bill McVey. NY City. 1954
viii	20th Century Fox Studios. 1966
9	Alan Rogers. NY City. 1957
10	Peter Gowland. Santa Monica. CA. 1959
16	Harry Langdon. Beverly Hills. CA. 1995
25	NY City. photographer unknown
26	Ziegfeld Follies of 1956. Shubert Theatre. Boston
32	Universal Pictures. Phipps Estate. Old Westbury. NY. 1995
34	Terry O'Neill. Shepperton Studios. London. 1969
41	Peter Basch. NY City. 1953
42	Harry Langdon. 1995
45	Thierry Mugler. AIDS Project Los Angeles. 1992
46-7	Harry Langdon. 1995
48	*Batman* TV series. Fox Studios. Los Angeles. 1967
49	Harry Langdon. 1995
51	Harry Langdon. 1995
53	Peter Gowland. Santa Monica. CA. 1982
58	Sidney Stafford. Stony Brook. NY. 1976
62	*Star Trek* TV series. Desilu. Los Angeles. 1968
	Batman TV series. 1966
63	*To Wong Foo. Thanks for Everything, Julie Newmar.* 1995
	Mackenna's Gold. 1969
64	Phillip Cohen. Los Angeles. 2010
66	Marilyn Martin. Chino. CA. 2010
67	Phillip Cohen. Los Angeles. 2010
68	Julie Newmar. Los Angeles. 1989
72	Sidney Stafford. Stony Brook. NY. 1976

Published by Eleven Books: **www.JulieNewmarWrites.com**
Julie Newmar Official Website: **www.JulieNewmar.com**

Designed by Cintia Martínez Delgado. Pablo Milberg and Julie Newmar.
Cover Design by Hushi Mortezaie. Mavis Kuo-Crary of Trash and Luxury and Ben Zhu of Nucleus Gallery.
Digital Finishing by Mariel Vega.
Edited by Robin Quinn.

ISBN 978-1-4507-3146-1

Self-Help   Inspiration   Celebrity

The Conscious

CATWOMAN

Explains

Life

on

Earth

The new last HOW-TO book

To my brother John who turned on the light

To my son John who is the light

Table of Contents

Acknowledgments

My profound thanks:

... to the mesmerizing *Pablo Milberg* – Argentinean web master
for shaping my words and photographs into mirth and wonder.

... to *Gregory Dean* – for making me love the computer
past a dozen failed attempts.

... to *David Wills* – photo-archivist, my tall
Australian friend who sat most agreeably
on the floor with me winnowing slides and
stills from two large drawers making this
lifetime of mine visually accessible
(out black spots and murky backgrounds!).

... to *Robin Quinn* – editor, as I
sashay meaning and content
past her sharp mind.

... to *Hushi Mortezaie* and *Mavis Kuo-Crary* –
for eliminating a kaleidoscope
of overhyped pictures into one fine cover.

... to *Ben Zhu* – Nucleus Art Gallery owner
for being the cool connoisseur
of great graphic design.

... to my brother *John Newmeyer* –
the smartest person I know and for suffering
the frequent phone calls in order to detangle
my fractured English.

All of us together
managed to achieve that charmed
– this is it! – moment.
That plateau from which to do even better.
I cherish our collaborative caper.
    These are the best days of my life.

Introduction
by *Janet Shapan*

A fine dictionary, a paperback on how to mend and repair things, and a personal diary qualify as items in my treasured library. Over the years, my favorites have become a collection of *"how to"* books. How to do just about anything and, of course, how to improve my life in 1001 ways.

It seems that growing up was a lot easier when I was a teenager. The thoughts of needing to be richer or prettier were of little concern, and as for being self-centered, it would never have been tolerated by my parents. It was also a special time because that happened to be an era when women were experiencing new freedoms, such as the pursuit of an advanced education and a professional career. Becoming a self-reliant *"how to"* woman was definitely an evolution of the mind, body and spirit in a way that had never been conceived of until that time.

Over the years, many of us may have forgotten the day-to-day details, but what we do remember vividly is the *"how to"* and self-help books we shared with each other. All the wonderful bits of information and inspirational words we cut out and put on our refrigerator doors and medicine cabinets.

As all young people do, we also searched for role models who defined the vision of our future selves. And we set our minds on emulating them. Finding myself to be gangly and much taller than my peers, it was Julie Newmar, the tall, statuesque, graceful and powerful woman, who inspired me. I was never going to be a cute beach bunny but I could be a little like Julie Newmar.

I rarely missed an episode of *My Living Doll* or *Batman*, and very few of Julie's other TV and movie performances over the years. Beyond the perfect exterior, I sensed the quality woman within her. I knew Julie's beauty had to be more than just skin deep, and I hoped someday I would have the opportunity to meet her and confirm my assumption. Not long ago, we did meet, and she showed me a copy of this manuscript.

Reading the book, I sat in great awe of the woman I had so admired all those years. I read a phrase and paused… read another phrase and took a breath… read more and cried once in a while. I found it to be a compilation of wonderful bits of information, inspirational thoughts, and practical advice for daily living that Julie has collected and experienced over her lifetime, and she was sharing it with me. It was an answer to my search for that perfect little *"how to"* book to place on my bedside table – the one that would empower me to be the very best I can be.

chapter one

How to have what you want...
including the impossible

I am not what I was, I am what I am,
I am more than what I was.

You are adored.
You are something that no one else is.
Forever and ever.

Drink the water from the glass half full or you'll go thirsty.

Move away from those who "can't" or "won't."
Be selective of whom you surround yourself with.

Put love into all things, most particularly
the impossible – especially the impossible.

If you dream it, you should have it. So that the next
dream can take its place. That's important.

Teach yourself, by writing to yourself.
Keep writing; very soon, something pops out.

If you want something, ask for it.
If you don't have what you want,
you've been going to the wrong source.
Think about that for twenty minutes.

The important thing is
to ask the right question.
Never mind the answer,
it will drop in your lap.

P R A Y E R   I S   P U R E   G O L D

If you knew how easy
it is to click your mental antennae
into the Infinite Mind, you'd discover
for yourself the secret of inspiration.
And it's free – for healing physical and mental problems,
reversing bad luck, anxiety, lack of education.

Don't be so busy. Find your own company.
Then to be creative – breathe a higher thought.
Whatever thought you're having, visibly see it
and breathe it to a higher level. Widen the space
you're thinking in, take another deep breath, and let it float up.
Free your mind from what you've learned and let it
enter the unknown. Free yourself from the experience,
then ask a big question and keep it floating up.
Find out for yourself. This time, be free of formulas.

Breathe yourself into the solution. Ask for "it."
It will come to you on your way to the gym.

Write it down. When I'm writing,
I half-close my eyes: it pulls up the deeper thought.
More than not, I usually have by 9 AM
what I've wished for or it has become
so clear to me how to get it.
Sometimes the phone rings with
an offer of a job, acceptance of a project.

Some people live to eat.
I write to know.
I write, therefore I know.

You are a light being,
anchored to Earth with your body.
Believe the highest thought about yourself
and you'll be where the action is right
for you. Besides, as Warren Buffett says,
you only need two or three big wins
in a lifetime.

If you practice any emotion, practice **joy**,
for that is your most natural state.
It's right up there next to love; your final step in life.
You can't be deprived of joy anyway, just give it more space.
Then let go in that space where you are momentarily healed
of everything, in perfect peace. Joy, as you'll see, is easily remunerated.

Breathe, consciously, slowly, deeply, and
your intelligence will open up like a fine lens.

I sometimes say to myself silently: "I can, I can, I can..."

Sammy Davis did it. Look at his odds!

Are you not as worthwhile as the President of the United States?
Well, why not? You are.

> You are no bigger or smaller
> than another human being.
> just not awakened enough.

How to *do* the impossible

One step at a time. One half-step, one quarter-step.
You'll be amazed, given time, how far you've gone.
Never give up: concentrate on the little things. Fear will be less noticed.

If you love what you do, then work is for idiots.
I've never worked a day in my life – never expect to.

"Working," however, is life's salvation. It makes
the leftover time, the cream, taste so sweet.

S A Y   " Y E S "   T O   N O W.

If you don't want to be first,
take more time and be best,
like Estée Lauder.

"First things first, but not necessarily in that order."
~ Bob Levey, *Washington Post*

THIRD-CENTURY DYNAMICS — DUMP THE DRECK.

Fill friction with love
and you will have healed
your part of the world.

3

Never, ever put yourself down; depressions are too hard to climb out of.

There are some people attached to their suffering and by repetition encourage its renewal. Enough is never enough.

"Treat your enemy as if one day he will become your friend."
~ *Publilius Syrus*

Accommodate, don't judge, or you may
have to go back and learn that other person's lesson.

Arrogance, ignorance,
Ignorance, arrogance.

On problem solving

Put your anger in a helicopter,
and feel yourself go up, up, up
– high enough until you
can see the "dynamics"
of the problem.

How much of it is petty stuff?
No longer worth your energy!

Most "isms" involve
one group stepping on another to feel equal.

So you made a mistake...
Was the action from love – or was it from fear?

Don't sin against yourself; collect thank-yous.

I like aggressors; they make me do things
I might not have done... and enjoyed.

N o t   " I   w i l l "   . . .   " I   c a n . "
For willing is always the future; **"I can"** is now.

Notice when you're seeking power over others.
and thus further obscuring your own ignorance.
Real power isn't ignorance.

Listen to your feelings.
Be aware of the sponsoring thought.
Is it from love or is it from fear?

I love flying over the Grand Canyon:
being so high above this
phenomenal creation
of life. earth. and water.
It gives me a peerless
perspective of my own and
the world's problems.

Responsibility is the home base
of great women and men.
Greatness requires taking responsibility for your feelings. your acts.
and their consequences.

Lack of responsibility lands you
in the hospital. the poor house.
or with "friends" who hurt you.

Winning is in the gut and achievable at any age
if one is able to challenge the unknown –
to fall upward. to precipitously dare from within.
Later in life. it's as if one must go small to be big.

Become ordinary.
Go against thought to that cherished level of personal grace.
Clint Eastwood has it.

Give... what you desire most.
Life's a circle, an echo; it all comes back.

It is pure self-deception to be complaining about what you're getting.
Be at cause. Seize the power.

Love everything you do and the likelihood is that it will
work so well that the unwanted will drop away faster,
leaving precious space for more of all that you do want.

Once you acknowledge limitation, have the guts
to expose to yourself your own meanness, pettiness,
or cruelty, and release its projection on others.
You will have planted the seeds of your own greatness.

"Force without wisdom falls of its own weight."
~ Horace

Be in the trust banking
business. Don't speak ill
of another, encouraging
holes in your bank
account for others
to rob you.

There is opportunity
in everything.
Everything.

Sorry
about
that,
but
it's
true.

Dream,
think,
act...
not the reverse.

Regrets;
the bruises of
often trying too hard.
Let regret fire you
up for the opportu-
nity that's just
now happening.

Society
is a big soup,
the better
for its
variety.

The *virtues* of failure

Mistakes? Forget it. Mistakes can be meteors to success.
Always ask. "What do I have to learn from this?"

If the problem **is** too big and it's a cruddy morning,
do only the small things. Clean a drawer, a closet.
Accomplishment will always,
always make you feel better.

If you could see that your strangeness,
your uniqueness, is exactly
what's right about you,
you'd give it all you've got.

To go up, you'll go down. Experience both.
One feels good, the other bad.
You need both... to be a safe person.

So be afraid. Get more of less.
Put being... before doing.
Think of a tightrope walker.

Success is a most desirable *disease.*

Be a 360-degree person
– imagine yourself seeing everything.
Imagine... to have lived God's plan
instead of your own.

Don't be afraid of your enemy.
His secrets are often most apparent.

In a negative situation, you must be more
than someone else's mirror and merely squawk.
The least you can do is turn your back
and walk away with love rather than rebuke.

Stuff happens.
So what!

ON CRITICIZING OTHERS

Don't hear it,
see it, or
respond to it
unless
you're in
an outdoor cafe,
Via Veneto style
and then
it's
prodigious
fun!

Only a brave Soul
can stand with the truth.
The rest of us
are too embarrassed
by our own ignorance
or poor experience.

Therefore,
stand back from dissidence
in order to understand
why it's even there.

chapter two

Why you are here...
the *divine gift*

Joy is the key to all life. It just is.

Sense, savor your own greatness; you will never come again, ever.

K.I.S.S.
Keep It Simple Stupid.
Simplify, you'll be closer to your truth.

Listen to your inner voice.
Be wrong or be right.
Pretty soon, you'll be right more of the time.

Be *authentic.*
Ask... does that feel real?

"If you've been noticeably living in the past,
ask yourself for a new image, one that has something to offer."
~ *Ruth Bettleheim, PhD*

Now, not then or when.
(That's easy for brilliant people like
Mel Brooks to do. He took on Hitler.)

There are times when you don't want, don't have to believe in you.
Believe in the infinite thread that connects you
to some unexplored whole and let go – then follow the wonderment.

Life works once you get to be more in a state
of gratitude than supplication or neediness.

The Spirit, the life inside you, is sacred. Ignore it at your peril.
Destroy it and it will haunt you.

How nice this world is... temporarily... for the bimbos and the arrogant.
Never mind, your Maker loves us all.

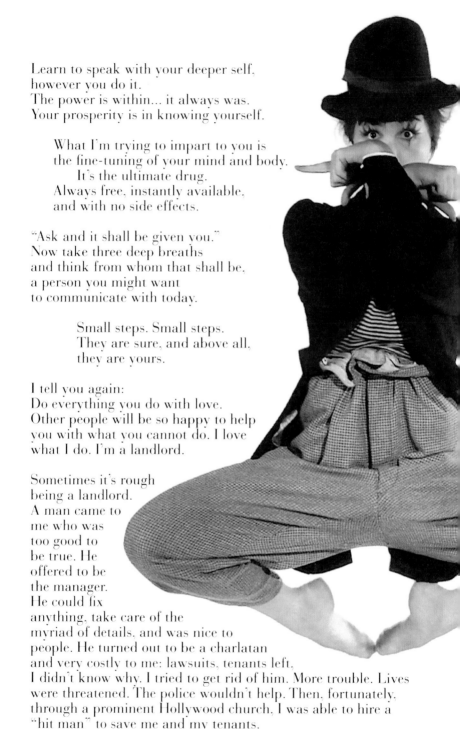

Learn to speak with your deeper self,
however you do it.
The power is within... it always was.
Your prosperity is in knowing yourself.

What I'm trying to impart to you is
the fine-tuning of your mind and body.
It's the ultimate drug.
Always free, instantly available,
and with no side effects.

"Ask and it shall be given you."
Now take three deep breaths
and think from whom that shall be,
a person you might want
to communicate with today.

Small steps. Small steps.
They are sure, and above all,
they are yours.

I tell you again:
Do everything you do with love.
Other people will be so happy to help
you with what you cannot do. I love
what I do. I'm a landlord.

Sometimes it's rough
being a landlord.
A man came to
me who was
too good to
be true. He
offered to be
the manager.
He could fix
anything, take care of the
myriad of details, and was nice to
people. He turned out to be a charlatan
and very costly to me: lawsuits, tenants left.
I didn't know why. I tried to get rid of him. More trouble. Lives
were threatened. The police wouldn't help. Then, fortunately,
through a prominent Hollywood church, I was able to hire a
"hit man" to save me and my tenants.
Not everything is as it seems.

Your ultimate dream

Yes, get to that goal. Why?
Because there are so many more goals beyond that.
Get used to the fast track.

If you can't follow your inner voice, at least note it down:
that way you'll have a jump on the journey.

Don't just use people.
Be sure you fit into another person's dreams. Ask.
Get what you want by assisting each other's dreams.

Love your mother. You asked for her.

Get mad, too.
Your parents were there to facilitate you
getting to your life's goal.

Have faith in your ability to know.

Your reward?
Doing it.

Whoever says it's too late is mentally standing
in a line that ended yesterday.

**Use intention
to empower your life.**

Before going to sleep or getting up in the morning,
give yourself an intention for the day.
Before having an important meeting
or phone call, use intention.

I use it before going to a party.
To do it, allow a thought to come to you
of the highest good to make
the particular event successful.

Yes, Yes, Yes.
Do what you love.
What your hand turns to.

Please God by doing great work in secret;
the rest will come easily.

"If you don't need prayer,
you haven't gone far enough."
~ *Dr. Robert H. Schuller*

When you have an impulse,
grab onto it:
it's opportunity knocking,
where your next move could be
– your new life, a better relationship.
Acknowledge your impulses.

Everyone has something to give. Give it.
It's the source of all riches.
If you're out of focus, see a psychiatrist:
take your mind to the cleaners.

The Infinite Mind always says "yes" to everything.
That's why it's important to be careful what you wish for,
what you talk about, and what you think about.

Your Maker is incomprehensibly smarter than you are and knows
what you need and the way you need it for your development.

Words, thoughts, eventually have a life of their own.
Never say something you don't want to be true.

**"One's eyes are what one is;
one's mouth what one becomes."**
~ *John Galsworthy*

It's important to stay on top of your dreams, the preludes
to what you want. Teach yourself by way of writing to yourself.
Very soon... something emerges you'll need to know.
I cannot tell you how important it is to have your gift in hand, in
front of your eyes, written down as words. You're halfway there then.
Even if you lose your grocery list, it's halfway there, by intention;
when you go to the store, it's not just lurking somewhere out of sight,
in the back of your mind. Unaccomplished.

Your dreamer comes first... your thinker second. Write it out – take
the most important third step. Then Do It!

> The purpose in life –
> and most wholesome it is –
> is to experience fullest glory.

Imagination...
all the way to *extraordinary*

Be still more often.
Don't bombard your ear and brain every minute.
Give Soul a chance to percolate to the surface of your awareness.

To make discovery unique... get lost.

Imagine a trip to heaven and your own life as a movie.
Make it great... now for an audience of one. Why?
Because we are all one.

We exist in our imagination of ourselves.

What is your vocation?
What does your hand reach for?
Follow it. It may be your next career.

Instincts... are subliminal feelings.
Emotions... are family stuff.
Trust your instincts... they have longer lineage.

chapter three

The great teacher...
an *inside* secret

"Here I am, fifty-eight, and I still don't
know what I'm going to be when I grow up."
~ *Peter Drucker*

Peace on earth starts within.

You'll notice that I tell you to breathe a lot.
You'll have the keys to all your safe deposit boxes,
some locked in fear, some with memories,
some with treasures.
The reason is to stay transparent,
out of heavy mass;
don't sink to the bottom.
If you're dealing with facts,
loose data, information under- or
over-load, then sleep on it.
Let the subconscious slow-cook it up
to the surface overnight.
Give your mind the best ingredients though;
then set it on "Resolve this, please."

Expect results.
Give yourself three nights for a big decision.

To get answers,
send yourself a mental letter.

The Spirit, the life inside you, is sacred.
Ignore it at your peril.

Be sure to open your heart
to this giant computer "post office"
of your subconscious.

The answer will drift in by midday,
during some routine task – while driving –
giving you solutions.

One of the most important things I taught myself was to become
my own teacher, leader, father, mother, even child.
From this point on, you cannot lose, because this time around
you become the parent you've always wanted, as well as
the child for whom infinite patience is at last received.
And you, as your pupil, can ask any question imaginable
because you, the teacher, the one with the most
unconditional love, is listening and wants
more than anything else
for you to succeed.

I urge you to have and do this – to give the very
thing to yourself you've always wanted.
Because there may have been bridges
you did not cross in your growing up
which were monumental
when you first encountered them... and faltered.
And whoever was there during that first failure
became the stone on which you trip at each
reencounter, be it public speaking,
handling money, or in relationships.

**Here lie the sources of your allergies,
the *who* – not the *what* –
you're allergic to...**

The mother who made normal life
so difficult for you.
Notice the abandoned person
who walks in the street;
such were his first encounters,
being abandoned
– it's what he knows.
The familiarity he's practiced
so earnestly is still in his life.

You can change things in you
but not in him,
by lovingly observing
each problem.

Here's an example...

I grew up in a home where money was never talked about by
my mother, rarely by my father, and only with great anxiety.
I never had an allowance and what "I needed"
was always provided. Money was a "no thing," like a penis,
something I didn't have.

One day, in my fifties,
I was sitting at my desk,
having struggled

for several years at UCLA night school,
through dozens of hours of business and
financial management, never liking arithmetic.
In what was either a flash of insight or
perpetual exhaustion, I used my right hand
to stroke the back of my left hand,
ever so gently, saying to myself:
"That's a good girl:
you made change so well,"
as if I'd been three or four years old
at a grocery store, receiving the approbation and
support from the unconditionally loving parent I had not experienced
at that crucial moment in life. In other words, this is when I became
my own parent and changed things forevermore.
Mind you, I'm not perfect, but I'm miles beyond
the financial cripple I was before.

At this moment, I wholly discovered the possibility
of parenting myself, of becoming my own guide and teacher.
No one knows as much as you do about what your needs are,
and this time you can give it to yourself – with the unconditional love
you need to become successful. Therefore,

re-parent yourself.

Don't make genes your excuse.

Everyone needs a mother.
Not necessarily yours!

If you can't think of it – then you can't have it.
It takes huge will, huge determination, to really have.

Relaxation. Concentration. The road to mastery.

One has to reach for something greater. One has to be in that space.
Now let go... to hold your magnificence, feel it, sustain it,
get whole with it, really familiar with it.

H a r m o n y   i s   a   b r e a t h   a w a y .   B r e a t h e .

I love Buckminster Fuller for saying,
"EVERYONE IS A GENIUS."

Everyone is a genius. My son John
has half the IQ of anyone reading this book:
it's just that he's higher up
on what Elisabeth Kübler-Ross calls
"the soul quadrant of life."
He is my teacher. And he doesn't say a word.

"You cannot truly listen to anyone
and do anything else at the same time."
~ *M. Scott Peck*

The amazing derring-do
to greatness is
inner listening.
Strange as it may seem,
you just may need
your own railroad
track in life.
A personal jet stream
wouldn't be bad.

What is greatness?
If you don't think
you have it, you haven't
kept the right company.
Fire everybody.

Don't ask, "Are you my boss, are you my friend?"
At least keep a clear path ahead of you so that
when the "information" comes, you're not attached.
What information? This is the part you train yourself to hear.

"Set aside all authority completely and totally."
~ *Krishnamurti*

To my Secret Partner:

Let me be able to observe that which is, with calmness,
then get me to the Truth, and let me feel Your direction.

On your area of intractable pain:

Again, this most likely comes from childhood.
Here lies your mental burial ground of hurts so deep,
created when you were young and helpless.
For protection, you pounded these feelings
out of sight, to a secret safer place.
Later they emerged as pain or disconnected anger.
These hurts are grounds for the success
of so many therapies.
But you can deal with them one by one,
until you don't hurt anymore.
You have the resources to do just that.

The action of doing this
will gradually reward you
with internal power,
the really BIG power,
and your physical illnesses
will just slip away.
You'll actually
get healthier
as you get older.

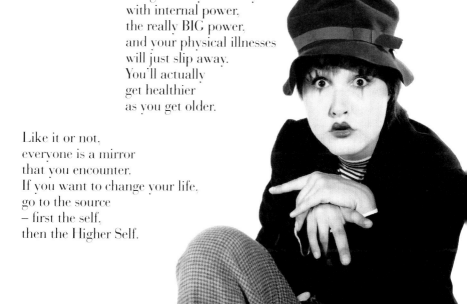

Like it or not,
everyone is a mirror
that you encounter.
If you want to change your life,
go to the source
– first the self,
then the Higher Self.

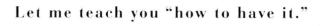

Let me teach you "how to have it."

1. Pick a problem, a want, or a worry.

2. Get paper and a pencil.
   Legal-size pads are my favorite.

3. Have a quiet space. No noise, music,
   voices, or time demands on you.
   Paying attention is high-energy
   business. I prefer early morning.

4. Sit comfortably, back straight,
   legs uncrossed. No distractions.

5. Slowly take as many deep breaths as you
   need. Be aware only of your chest/lungs
   breathing. Gently close your eyes. Let go of
   thinking. The breathing energizes your
   mind. See each breath pumping this
   energy up, up, up to a satellite, a place
   we will call Infinite Mind.
   Think of each breath as
   fine-tuning your receiver-radio
   to the big power station up above.

   Now, ask yourself:
   "What do I want to work on?"
   Write it down.

   Write it so it's clear.
   Write it again, until it is clearer still.
   Write it again til it's absolutely clear.
   Keep it simple.
   Keep breathing...
   Look at the words...

Allow whatever comes to your
hand and write that down,
no matter what.

**Breathe,
write the next thing.
Keep breathing.**

By the fifth or eighth sentence, you may
hit upon the clarity that you need.
Keep writing until you feel "filled";
you'll know. Trust yourself.

Keep doing it.

It's not about writing;
it's about pulling up
subconscious knowledge. Everything you want to know is there,
and you'll be told where to get it or
how to find it.

I reiterate… This is creation.
Be in absolute freedom.
Very important, **allowing.**

Now ask yourself
that question you've been
seeking the answer for.

Have calm
awareness.
Ask it again.

Breathe.

Keep clarifying
the question.

**In the question
is the answer.**

Put kindness into the little things.
The way you give direction is a perfect example.
Be in the other person's mind.

**Give more than you receive.
You'll attract enough of your own kind
who will do the same for you.**

Receive. Life is a relay;
receive it, then turn it over.
Get the rush, get the flow.

Notice what's genuinely good
under the surface of another.
Feel his goal and uncover it to him.
You will be loved forever.

**Don't lie, or a rung on
your ladder will give way.**

Contribute only value in this world
or let someone else do it.

Have integrity.
Be a safe person to be with.
Don't rend holes in the safety net
or your loved ones will fall
through.

Live life with gratitude and gifts will flow in.

Adversity is there to advance you...
Nothing more.

To cry is sometimes
sublimely joyful;
the pain is up and out,
and now there's a place
to move forward in.

Your time is now, no matter what, who, or how.

"I can."   **(I love that statement.)**

chapter four

Energy *versus* fatigue

*Get used to every now and then
asking your body
what it needs or wants.
It will tell you... if you let it.
Let your body have a voice.*

"Nature cures."
~ *Voltaire*

Don't try to do it all
or you're depriving people of loving you.

For the morning blahs: When you're
feeling too rotten to work. work anyway!
Do the unimportant stuff first.
until you're out of the fog.
If that fails. sleep;
either your subconscious or your body
has some message that you've ignored:
that is nature's warning.
Often pain or distress goes away
in sleep. Don't feel guilty
about the refurbishment of rest.

"To every thing. there is a season..." ~ *Ecclesiastes 3:1*
(I am still understanding this.)

From doornail dead... to energy with power.
In 7 minutes.

Here is the formula that has saved my life. my energy.
my disposition. and probably my looks. The taste won't be high
on your list. I use it before a workout. for the 4 PM blahs.
even before I go to a party (I don't drink alcohol).
It works for major exhaustion when sugars. caffeine. and other
stimulants turn against you. This one builds your body and
sustains it naturally for hours. It is protein. the most important
known component of living matter.

1 heaping tablespoon liver powder
1 tablespoon spirulina
(Premix)

With just enough pineapple or Clamato juice
for only three to four swallows, wash it down with something yummy,
in 7-8 minutes the "slump" will be gone.
It energizes the mind and pumps a feeling of youth and vigor
into the body. Don't think of the taste, watch the results.
It never fails. All-night sex… well?

Pain... Anger... Fear...
Cursing, Craziness & Compulsions

While you're young, go crazy every once in a while... It clears the air.

Idealism promotes order over chaos, at whose expense?
Not mine, please. On the other hand, if I'm the one in chaos,
I try to keep my distance... til order prevails.

**Alcohol? Parties?
Love yourself.
Go home in one piece.**

"Who would desire peace
should be prepared for war."
~ *Vegetius*

On people you hate
or have a great problem with:

Get real or get off it.
What qualities in the other person
do you fear, fear you're lacking,
or felt deprived of earlier in your life?
Get some of it.
You're more likely to hate
what you don't have than what you have.
Life has many notes.
A piano has eighty-eight keys;
don't just use fourteen.

Never curse God: She-He's the big boomerang.
You might as well run downhill on a slippery slope.
You're asking for it.

Look for the real feeling underneath the curse you just made.

There's always AA.

To overcome my early teen insecurities, I took to heart Dale Carnegie's *How to Win Friends and Influence People.* I venture to say this book took my mind on a crusade for life.

Reacting...
& Staying Cool

Watch out for fear of anything.
It carries too many downsides.
It also sells a lot of medicine.
And will empty your pockets.

"I am not afraid,
I am not afraid,
I am not afraid."
One of the best mantras.

On compulsions

Maybe the only compulsion I have is to be different.
No amount of psychological arm-twisting
has changed me. I still love being different.
Then again, I don't particularly mind loneliness,
being late, being outside,
not knowing what's going on.
Maybe I'd better change this and
become short, fat, and popular.

In order to understand what's going on around you, in your house, business, or part of the world, imagine yourself riding above the energy that's there. Most people become the energy, then get into fights about right and wrong, which never can be won. Drop it. See the dynamics, be an observer, ride above it so that you can get the wave of the future.

COOL

Detachment: Removal of self,
chosen non-partisanship, coolness.
Let the other guy go for the grief.
Being the third party out of the
argument; on top of, looking down.
Able to change the subject;
go home, get positive.

Detached: Unconcerned about
mere trauma, goading,
unnecessary sensitivity.
Breathing from the belly,
relaxed in your extremities,
your hands and eyeballs
plainly knowing better
things to do.

The difference
between a
leaf blower
and a
broom.

**Fast refocus; rise above it.
Practice this...
and stay away from losers.**

chapter five

How to *improve* on your parents

Teach yourself.

"Home is not where you live, but where they understand you."
~ *Christian Morgenstern*

**"Nothing has a stronger influence on children
than the unlived life of the parents."**
~ *Carl Jung*

Applaud the little successes in people: be patient with the rest.

Expectations... a sure direction toward divorce.

Be pleased you are shy in your early years.
Let other people make the mistakes first.
No matter how much you yearn to be a leader,
your time may not have come yet. It will.

Firstborns make the mistakes that their younger siblings learn from.

Assumptions... a sure way to be out of step, or offend another.

"No matter how many communes anybody invents,
the family always creeps back."
~ *Margaret Mead*

Parents: Did you have the wrong ones?
Again, the secret is... to become your own parent.
Stop looking for one in your husband or special other.
Don't try to remake anybody.

Doing things gently and kindly builds a bridge to anywhere.

Everyone needs a grandmother.
Food, love... the first three years.

To have a child at any age is to have a treasure.
If, uppermost, that child is conceived preeminently out of profound
love, it has the greatest chance of having the best of all possible worlds.

chapter six

Rich... Or *really* rich?

Appreciation... Give it away.

It's not what you do but how you do it...

Every profession has its scullery duty.

No matter how much money you make,
it's worthless when you leave.

Making money is like going to the bathroom; it feels so good.
You laugh, but it truly is the manure test.
Spread it around, you know, for young ideas to grow.

**"A good reputation is more valuable than money.
Everything is worth what its purchaser will pay for it.
In every enterprise, consider where you would come out."**
~ *Publilius Syrus*

Do you really want beauty,
wealth or intelligence?
Be advised, it is a big responsibility.
It'll make you humble. If not,
you don't have it; it has you.

"Sicilian tyrants never invented
a greater torment than envy."
~ *Horace, Epistles, Book I*

Not being able to receive
limits financial security.
Does it ever!

Notice...
What you are pretending to have.
If you pretend that you have no power,
what do you think will happen?

Happiness, for me, used to be having things.
Now it's more a balance of it all –
not too much food, money, possessions, but enough –
as well as not being in fear of not having enough.

The license plate: "Ur a Luv"
was on the back of a gentleman's custom-made convertible.
No wonder he was rich.

You have no idea how much people love you.
Write or receive a fan letter; that way, you'll see.

"The sleep of a laboring man is sweet
but the abundance of the rich
will not suffer (allow)
him to sleep."
~ *Ecclesiastes 5:12*

Zero Mostel in *Monsieur Le Coq*

chapter seven

Taste – How to have it…
in *3 to 6* seconds

CLOTHES, HOUSES, FRIENDS

"Your physical appearance is the front door to your life."
~ Madelyn Whiting

I hide my annoyance when people tell me:
"But you can wear anything!"
Anything is what I don't wear.

I feel a little bit guilty about fooling the world.
If they only knew how many rehearsals it takes
to walk confidently. Even my bathing suits, leotards,
cat suits are fit to the purpose of
"ac-cent-uate the positive... e-lim-inate the negative."

When entering a restaurant: Drop the attitude.
People have too much attitude
these days, a lot of it mendacious.
Just put one foot quietly
in front of the other.

BE LIGHT OF SPIRIT.

Great people make you feel greater.
Petty people make you feel smaller.
Now you know who
to hang out with.

Organize.
The seeds
of progress
await you
in organization.

Tidiness reaffirms purpose.
It conditions mentality.

How to have great taste in clothes... it's easy:

Stand before a well-lit mirror having outdoor light.
Choose the one thing you want to wear that day,
even if it's your comfortable shoes.
Have all your other choices ready
to hold up in front of the mirror.
Now... the trick is to half-close your eyes as you look
(fewer distractions that way).
Get your gut feeling of good, better, or best,
that the mirror will tell you.

Or use my sound test of grunts or ah-hahs.
Guttural sounds are an excellent rating
system for anything that requires
taste, judgment, discernment;
it can be applied to people's behavior,
or for trusting another.

First impulses
are hugely important.
You often don't get or give
a second chance.
Trust your gut...
your half-closed eyes.

To critique a picture or
photograph, turn it upside down.
The secrets fall out.

"It's amazing how potent cheap music can be."
~ *Noel Coward*

Color is music to the eyes...

Sounds attract and repel.
They bother you or vibrate sensation straight to your heart,
as the blue-violet color of a tanzanite gemstone does to me.

I have a memory for 10,000 colors.
I also have perfect pitch.
My friends are either extremely pleased
or extremely annoyed with me.

How to remember to do things:

Immediately throw any object at hand on the
floor, preferably in a doorway, which then
becomes your obstacle for recall.
"What's that doing there?"
As you leave the room:
"Ah, yes..."

How to find really lost things:

Sit for a moment quietly.
Focus on the object.
Allow a feeling to come
to your hand...
of a direction...
to a warm spot.
Follow it.
It's not so much your
brain, but your hand
that has a memory of
where you last put
what's "lost."
Never allow frustration
or the words "I can't"
to keep you from finding it.

On good manners:

Good manners are wisdom
practiced backwards.
Bad manners are the throne
of selfishness claiming
to be individuality.
Road rage, plane rage,
and drunkenness
being irreversible selfishness.

Learn all the rules first, then,
if you wish, break them.
Be natural. To be safe, be appropriate.

"I changed... in order to not be the same,"
noted a snake as he shed his skin.

How to have a designer's taste or re-do your best friend's house:

1. Stand back from the area that needs improvement.

2. Half-close your eyes;
   this gets rid of distractions and your friend.

3. Breathe and mumble your response without her hearing it.
   Give it a grade from 1 to 10 by making, thus,
   certain severities of sounds; a guttural utterance is good.

4. Tell her your plan.

5. Chances are you're right – for where you are in
   your own development, not hers, of course.

6. Look for a new friend.

chapter eight

Treasuring... yourself

Treasure yourself... do nothing less.

Then you will have cultivated the talent of treasuring others:
Instinct will give you the rest.
Make others millionaires and
you will not have to work a day in your life.

Treasure... the things you love.

Get them out of the drawers. from behind the cabinets.
Set them out front and center. Feel the "lift" they give your life.

"I believe in person to person: every person is Christ for me. and
since there is only one Jesus. that person is the one person
in the world at that moment."
~ *Mother Theresa*

You cannot fail; you just need more practice.
Rehearse anything important.
Rehearsal gives spontaneity underlying confidence.

I like short people. They make me feel big.
It's the people that doubt their existence
that are dangerous.

The delicacy and receptivity of thought
have a lot to do with why so many females
are in the intuitive mind arena.
This is our power –
as it guides, calms and restores.

FORGIVE YOURSELF FIRST

You'll have reserves when you want others to forgive you.

I'm surprised how many people like me.
Is this distance. ignorance.
or am I getting somewhere?

To a person whose sense of identity is wispy:
Don't forget to validate yourself.

To be alone is bliss. Is it possible I have found myself?

Women bloom later in life. Some of them,
like roses, bloom, and rebloom and rebloom.

I hate noise.
Is it because
my son is deaf?

"What cannot be removed
becomes lighter
through patience."
~ *Horace*

E x p o s i n g . . . Y o u r s e l f

Attack the attacker in yourself... expose yourself and your fears.
If necessary, even get professional mental help.
You'll be less dangerous in society and not have the feeling of
constantly falling out of a wall-less building.

The way to gain power and accomplishment is by knowing yourself first.

Let go, fall on your face.
What you learn from the experience will make you 10 feet taller.

"When a man realizes his littleness, his greatness will appear."
~ *H.G. Wells*

"I've had more trouble with myself than any man I've ever met."
~ *Dwight Moody*

For years, I've had an aloof relationship to my ego, an empty space
where my ego should have been. Was that a price for being tall?

chapter nine

Beauty. The wrinkle on

Beauty is 1/3 natural, 1/3 spirit and 1/3 illusion.

> Don't be afraid of the latter.
> The world accepts it that way.

To teenagers:
> **Unless you are as smart as Barbra Streisand,
> you're too myopic to see your own beauty.**

Standards change every other year.
Thin lips, fat lips, piercings, tattoos, in, out,
natural bosom, pushed up, out.
Enhance but don't mess with nature.
Even a widow's peak hairline at one time
was the rage, and women had their hair
plucked out over their foreheads, while men
fight their own fears by combing whatever
they have forward.

Have the courage to measure yourself
in your Maker's eyes only.

> Don't try to be like others;
> you'll not only be sorry,
> you'll soon be out of fashion
> and the shallowness,
> the telltale marks of your
> insecurity, will show.

Don't ask anyone to be true to you, even
your best friend. You must be true to you.

F a k e r y   l e s s e n s   y o u.

> It's so hard in your teens to believe
> in yourself because you're quite
> simply not formed yet.
> So don't force it. Don't measure
> yourself to others; walk alone.

The only way to get through this time is to have good parents, good morals, good discipline.
Don't shortchange yourself by cheating.
You'll then have a real bank account from life to spend.

Be yourself;
Nature rejects the false.
You are enough.
Please remember you are enough.

Everyone's skin is different.

Mine requires only soap and water to clean it.
Looking under a microscope, the renowned cosmetician.
Erno Laszlo, discovered that skin has pore-clogging residues unless rinsed thirty times. My advice is to rinse at least fifteen times in clear warm water – three more in cold water to close the pores and get the glow.

To perk up the late afternoon tired look:
Splash hot water on your face two or three times:
it refreshes the complexion.
Works for men too.

For no wrinkles:
In her mid-sixties my mother had none.
I have none, probably because as a teenager she forbade me to lie in the sun like the other girls.

**How I broke
the habit of frowning**

Practice in front of a mirror some heavy frowning.
Frown and hold it as hard as you can. It needs to hurt and look really ugly to you.
You need to see how unattractive it is and to notice what muscles you're using.
Relax. Repeat three times.
Make a bad thing conscious.

Tall girls, don't slump.

> Think of how many short guys out there
> who would love to have your offspring.
> Stand up for them.

The perfect place to check your posture is in an elevator. Press your spine and head up against the backside wall, then walk away tall.

The Lift

> Use the cheek muscles to memorize the "Kegel" facelift:
> Smile within. Smile inside, lips closed – lift the cheeks.
> Singing taught me the cheek and mouth lift.
> Singers have a natural facelift, an apple-cheek smile.

Resist the urge to turn back the clock too much with plastic surgery.
The inner glow is more powerful because it comes
without neediness and without loss.
It's the one bank account that can't be depleted.

For a beautiful body and legs

> My top choice is ballet class,
> especially for girls
> from eight to thirteen.
> You'll get to skip
> that awkward stage;
> your body will have
> natural confidence.

> Ballet elongates the legs and
> gives you that lifetime perfect posture.
> It has actually made my feet
> one size smaller.

> You'll feel like a princess
> and be able to wear clothes
> that others envy.
> You'll be above the crowd.

The number-one exercise for tight hips and curvy legs is the plié.

1. Hold onto something stationary.

2. Feet apart, toes facing out.

3. Slowly bend knees halfway to floor.
Keep those heels down and your upper body straight.

4. Slowly straighten up. Repeat eight times.

5. Repeat this sequence three times.

Photography

The light of the body is the eye.
When having my picture taken,
I usually watch the photographer's finger,
anxiously seeking the shutter button;
for some reason, it always makes me laugh and I feel at ease.

To look thinner, turn one shoulder slightly back.
To have gorgeous legs and be taller... do a Marlene Dietrich;
she had photographers on their knees shooting up,
not from the head down making you look short and
dumpy, which the paparazzi does.

For a better face or portrait: Be sure the main light, your "key" light,
is in front of you, not overhead or way off to the side,
and no higher than 10 o'clock.
Tilt your chin slightly forward; Elizabeth Taylor does this.
Be animated from inside. Smile from behind your lips,
take a deep breath and think any thought with love or sex in it.

Why do blue eyes photograph best?
Because light draws and dark repels.

Go ahead, look right into the lens.
Be warned, the camera reads your mind.
It takes practice to look natural
in front of the camera.

Makeup...
Sometimes I just plain overdo it.

If so...
blot half your makeup off,
especially for the brightest
outdoor days.
Subtlety makes for success.

49

Makeup... trick & secrets

Spend all you want on lipstick: it's your premier weapon of attraction.
Put the darker color inside your lips.
and the lighter color outside. Subtle lip pencil can reshape the mouth.

Try an eye shadow that's halfway
between your eye color and your hair.
Gold and blue do mix.
Look for the undertones in your hair.
the secondary color of your eyes.
Mix colors – this underplays the beauty of your eyes.

For larger eyes. put the shadow
under as well as over the eye.
Softly smudge it. Keep practicing: it works.

For really large eyes. use an eyeliner on top of your shadow.
The secret is to keep the line 1/16 of an inch further away
from your lashes. with the exception of just over the pupil.
It takes courage and practice. Here is an illusion that works.

To arch or reshape your eyebrows.
use moustache wax from a theatrical makeup store.

Never put glitter on any part of your face or body
that you're not satisfied with.
No shiny noses. please.
I use French powdered papers (called Papier Poudre).

The one cream I could never do without –
pure hydrous lanolin
by the pound. from the drug store.

Most perfumes and colognes can't be kept over six months.
Get a second opinion before you frazzle the public
with your favorite scent.
It might be better as room spray.

Ninety percent of what I buy
becomes spray for the bathroom.

Black sheer stockings make legs slender, curvier, sexier.
Don't wear sheen hosiery: it distorts even gorgeous legs.

How to lengthen your leg:
Coco Chanel designed the perfect shoe.
Nude-color with a black toe,
worn with nude stockings.

Belts made of elastic are my favorite...
they accommodate lunch and sneak your waist in again afterwards.

The most attractive era for women's clothing, in my opinion,
was during World War II. The shoulders, skirt length,
waist, shoes, and hats were adorable. In spite of scarcities
of the time, women had strength and femininity.

As a woman,
I've always thought of myself as having power.
The power to command, the power to say "no,"
the power to manipulate, persuade, dissuade,
encourage, expand, evolve.

Intimate settings

After seeing myself on film,
I put these notes on my dressing table.
They are reminders to:

- Have a calm face.
- Take my time.
- Be centered...
  and listen.

- Relax the tension in my mouth.
- Don't be too cutesy or try to please.
- Don't fuss with clothes or
  makeup in public.

chapter ten

Health

**Illness is the body's wisdom of making you stop
so that you may realign your mind
toward the goal your Soul wants for you.**

Thinking sick thoughts
doesn't lead to better health.
What you think, you become.

"Stand porter at the door of thought."
~ *Mrs. Hazel Wright,*
my Sunday school teacher

It's almost funny how perfectly our bodies work,
even when they work imperfectly.
The body is like math, really.
Add up the numbers incorrectly
and who's to blame?
Not the numbers.

The body eventually does what the mind tells it to.
It's just that in many cases your body is far wiser than your mind is.
Let information travel the other way by listening to,
rather than immediately eliminating, your symptoms.

To make the world healthy, heal yourself...

If someone tells you they love you,
or embraces you,
soak it up like a blotter to a table full of spilt milk.
Receive all the good you can get.
Let it send a warm thrill through your body.
Stay with it.
This is the stuff that heals.

Hugging: your cells' best cleanser.

The body was created to work perfectly.
As your dad said, "If it's working, don't tinker with it."

Your body has a very high intelligence.
Its designer didn't come out with the Yugo car.

If you have realized an illness in your body,
it's probably there to save your life!
Illness is the attention-getter
that is now trying to force you to change or
stop doing something to yourself
that is hurting or limiting you.
Have you made a secret pact to team up
with a loved one who has passed on?
Your body may develop some hard-to-detect
or unknown disease.

New science reveals you can change your genes.

"Much is your environment, but much more is your perception.
Today's scientific dogma is as unexplored as the concept of the
flat fifteenth century earth. If you want to be well, break away
from this kind of certainty. You're not a random event.
The power of your thought emits an energy
quite beyond your body.
Don't give away your power.
Be at cause and not effect.
Don't throw yourself out of balance."

"The planet reflects where we are right now."
~ *Dr. Bruce Lipton, Cellular Biologist*

Respect the chain of command.
Soul travels faster than the speed of light.
Mind ticks off its thoughts in minutes.
The body's response to both is in days or years.
Therefore, when you see a need for change,
go upward with respect to cause.

On food:
How not to get too fat or too thin

1. First, learn the rules of nutrition.
   The desire for sweets can be overcome by eating enough protein.

2. "Forbidden" foods can be enjoyed if you take small bites
   and chew with passionate, undivided attention.

3. To kill the after-dinner desire for sweets, wait 20 minutes.
   Distract yourself. The desire is usually gone.

Golden Rule
Eat that which perishes fastest

When stressed,
look to the distance.
Look far out at the horizon,
and none of the waves
can make you sick.

Your mind tells you one thing
but what does your body say?

I purchase vitamins
as a form of life insurance.

If you want to be thought of
as beautiful.
have a restful face.

I am extremely
well
aged.

chapter eleven

Laughter, other thoughts and great thinkers

I noticed how happy I am and it was Sunday.

Walk in another's shoes and your feet hurt.

To make people laugh:
Tell the truth. Children do.
You can always apologize: laugh at your folly.
Have fun. Above all, be genuine.

What happened to nice children?
There are too many little "me-firsts" running around yelling
and mucking up our mental spaces.

"Old men are only walking hospitals."
~ *Horace*

Great people, like Lucille Ball and Desi Arnaz,
shine great praise on others.
Their creative bank increases with use,
and runneth over, to the rest of us.

Movie stars are misunderstood.

In general, most are highly intelligent.
Much of this intelligence is focused
on their egos.
Yet the ego is their product
like Saltines was Nabisco's...
Nabisco invested a lot of time
preserving that taste.
You wouldn't want a soggy Saltine.
If the star is able to separate himself from
his ego and care for it
like a product, he has a much better
chance of surviving intact.

The Kennedys always knew your name
before they met you. They genuinely
wanted to know about you and they all had
nonstop energy.   No wonder they attracted top talent.

Large people are so often gentle...
They hate being picked on.

Short men do everything twice. I like that.

My brother is a genius. And I like him.
Most smart people are quite calming to be around.
You don't have to take care of them.
I like being in the middle: a few smart people, a few runts.

My Junior High School teacher, Violet Walker,
was the teacher of teachers.
Her nobility of purpose gave me a solid anchor
for the rest of my life.

Noblesse Oblige = Christopher Reeve.

"My life is my message."
~ Gandhi

"Give strong drink unto him
that is ready to perish,
and wine unto those
that be of heavy hearts."
~ Proverbs 31:6

Thank Heaven for the needy,
and the needed; that's us.
Thank Heaven for nuns;
they give care to the unwanted.
Thank Heaven for eagles and
breeds of carrion eliminators.
Thank Heaven for I.F. Stone,
Handel...

"I shall not wholly die. What's
best of me shall 'scape the tomb."
~ Horace

Take inventory; you have enough talent for a lifetime.
In truth, you have more than enough.

Tell the truth; it will upgrade your audience.

Frederick Jackson on Julie Newmar:
   "She got more boys through puberty than anyone else on earth."

         "It is impossible to love and be wise."
               ~ *Frances Bacon*

      "I shall have more to say when I am dead."
            ~ *Edwin Arlington Robinson*

New York City enlivens your energy.
One revels in other people's achievements,
sometimes to the neglect of one's own.

      If you were born in Texas, get away for a while.

         California, especially Southern California,
         queers the pitch of Easterners,
         those on the intellectual front burner.
         This fuzzball of certitude serves to amuse us out West.
         Brains and bounty do need a coast of their own.

         Latin actors are somewhat over the verge.
         American actors are over-using "cool."
         Irony mostly leaves me cold.

As performers we overdo,
thus taking the experience away from the audience.
Sometimes it's enough just to say the words.
That's what British actors do.
And Clint Eastwood – for him,
one sentence is a whole movie.

   Carol Lombard was the perfect female movie star:
      bright, beautiful, playful and unself-conscious.

         We should not pity the Kennedys.
            They are no more cursed than we are.
      It's just that they have access to more expensive
               and destructive toys than we have.
            We all use poor judgment, make hasty,
      ill-informed decisions in our rush to success and adoration.

Besides, people of quality don't want to be pitied.

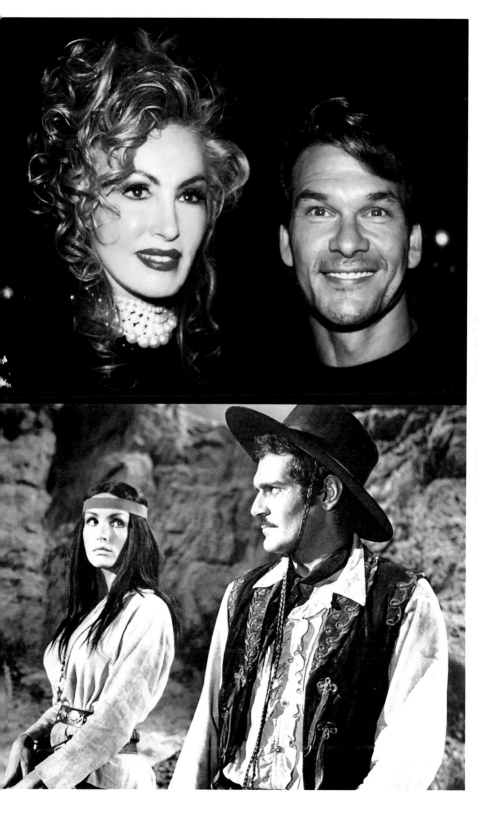

chapter twelve

Gardening
and world solutions

**"Finally, you understand that the real garden
you are working on is yourself."**
~ Robert M. Pirsig, Zen and the Art of Motorcycle Maintenance

Get up before dawn...
and every single songbird will welcome you to the world.

I try never to miss the quiet intelligence
of people who work with their hands.
Farmers are my favorite people.

"How fair is a garden amid the
trials and passions of existence."
~ Benjamin Disraeli

"Though an old man
I am but a young gardener."
~ Thomas Jefferson

No two days in my garden
are ever the same.

I love stones.
So much goes into so little.
There's a rockery in Kyoto, Japan
where landscapers go to get rocks
for their gardens.
Some of them cost as much as $250,000.
Like the Washington monument,
these rocks evoke power.

"I've never had so many good ideas
day after day as when
I worked in the garden."
~ John Erskine

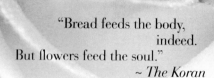

"Bread feeds the body,
indeed.
But flowers feed the soul."
~ *The Koran*

Julie Newmar
Rose

I garden, therefore I am.

You can bury a lot of troubles digging in the dirt.

Plant carrots in January and you'll never have to eat carrots.

An addiction to gardening is not all that bad
when you consider all the other choices in life.

"We can complain because rose bushes have thorns
or rejoice because thorn bushes have roses."
~ *Abraham Lincoln*

On yourself, as in a garden:
Weed the demons from the mind of nature.

"I'm not really a career person. Basically I'm a gardener."
~ *George Harrison*

Demand to be well! Go out and watch the flowers grow.
All sane formulas for living can be found in the garden.

When weeding, the best way to make sure you are removing a weed
and not a valuable plant is to pull on it.
If it comes out of the ground easily, it is a valuable plant.

God made rainy days
so gardeners could get the housework done.

A small house, a large garden... Heaven.

Julie Newmar
Daylily

John Jewl

chapter thirteen

The Book of Jewls
(my son's middle name)

The Ten Commandments are powerful rules
meant to save lives as the road gets narrower.
Should they be displayed in public?
Sure. but subtly. on an inside door or cabinet as a kind of safety net.
Go into your closet and pray. unless you're comfortable in wigs.
frou frou and runny mascara.

Most of what I know I experience through my ears.
I hear your condition in the tone of your voice.
even when you try to hide it.
If you don't want to share. I hear that too.

There are some people you have to chase all over the place.
They are deceivers. It's how they function.
I can't break it down. but they are very tiring.

Then there are some people I just adore.
They let you in. at least far enough: they offer trust.

A wonderful person came before them and
gave them trust. maybe a mother.
They are not forever attached to conspicuous mistakes.

The sweetest courage... is in being alone.

I strongly feel that real healers cannot practice malevolence.
It has been mine as well as universally experienced that
the Divine Intelligence works only for good.

Thanks to anybody who gets me to like
what I don't like.
see what I haven't seen.
or exposes opposition.

**"Be aware that each of us is doing
as well as he can at this moment."**
~ Madelyn Whiting

Exhortations to the self

We teach... in order to learn.

Warren Beatty's secret:
he never took his eyes off you and he never gave up.

"It takes a long time to become young."
~ *Picasso*

At a party, try innocence instead of sophistication.
It lessens the other person's competitiveness and
opens the heart for others to know you.

On stage fright:
There's no such thing.
It's the big energy you need to project out there
to that many people.
Be completely prepared and you'll have a wonderful time.
A wonderful time is what the audience came for.
Besides, you can't afford to project fear.
Fear makes people uncomfortable.
Take several deep breaths before you walk on stage.
It energizes you.
Then say, "I love you," several times
to your audience before they see you.

Being perfect makes me gripe all the time.
Imperfection is more satisfying.
And I have more friends.

No one worth possessing can be.

The very last word is love.
It's always love.
Use it in as many ways as possible.
Especially in regard to yourself while you're here.

My brother was an atheist at seven,
an agnostic at fourteen, and now he listens to Bach.
Is God inevitable?

When I first drove around in my pricey Porsche 928,
I noticed how young and carefree the other guy was in his jalopy.

I am looking for a friend, beautiful in my eyes,
tall or short, and playful as a dolphin.

I'd rather be
an artist
than a billionaire.
A millionaire is
alright.
I've already done that.

Death is a no thing.
I would just like
the drawer to be full
of my favorite things.

There's so much more to do.

About The Author

Actress, dancer, pianist, mime…
Born in Hollywood…
known for being the quintessential **Catwoman**.

Julie Newmar dropped out of college to become a choreographer / dance director for *Universal Studios*. Her early appearances are often seen on *YouTube*, including her role as the golden statue-come-to-life in the film *Serpent of the Nile*. She was next cast as one of the brides in the classic MGM musical, *Seven Brides for Seven Brothers*. Like her mother, a former Ziegfeld girl, Julie made the New York stage her next horizon at age 19.

She soon became an overnight sensation as the one and only Stupefyin' Jones in *Li'l Abner*. Julie would recreate the same role on Broadway 42 years later, in the same costume. Subsequent to the original performance, her legs were insured for 10 million dollars (not however, in the event of theft).

Julie won a Tony for her acting role on Broadway in the hit comedy *Marriage-Go-Round*, and she was immediately accepted by the prestigious *Actors Studio*. Loving dance, she continued to star in Bob Fosse's musicals on and off Broadway. She toured nationally with Joel Grey in *Stop the World I Want to Get Off*.

She guest-starred in many now-favorite TV episodes, on shows such as *The Monkees*, *Columbo*, *Love American Style*, *Get Smart*, *Star Trek*, *F Troop*, *The Beverly Hillbillies*, *Twilight Zone* and *Route 66*. The part she's most fondly remembered for is Catwoman, in the original *Batman* television series.

In 1995, *Universal Pictures* and *Steven Spielberg's Amblin Entertainment* produced a movie named after her, *To Wong Foo, Thanks For Everything! Julie Newmar*. In the film, Julie appeared as herself.

With cutting-edge sensibility, Julie retrained herself into the Internet world of social media. Active on *Facebook:* http://www.Facebook.com/JNewmar. **Julie** is currently working on four books, and various videos to be seen on the media section of her website, www.JulieNewmar.com.

An avid gardener, **Julie**'s gardens are renowned. There is a rose, daylily and begonia named after her. See: http://JulieNewmar.com/videos/julie_newmar_garden/

Julie has a handicapped son who *"sparks love and a high level of creativity"* in her life.

CPSIA information can be obtained
at www.ICGtesting.com
Printed in the USA
BVXC01n1346161014
370901BV00001B/5

* 9 7 8 1 4 5 0 7 3 1 4 6 1 *